A SHORTER LIFE

A SHORTER LIFE

Alan Jenkins

Chatto & Windus

LONDON

Published by Chatto & Windus 2005

2 4 6 8 10 9 7 5 3 1

First published in Great Britain in 2005 by
Chatto & Windus
Random House, 20 Vauxhall Bridge Road,
London SW1V 2SA

Random House Australia (Pty) Limited
20 Alfred Street, Milsons Point, Sydney,
New South Wales 2061, Australia

Random House New Zealand Limited
18 Poland Road, Glenfield,
Auckland 10, New Zealand

Random House (Pty) Limited
Endulini, 5A Jubilee Road, Parktown 2193, South Africa

The Random House Group Limited Reg. No. 954009
www.randomhouse.co.uk

A CIP catalogue record for this book
is available from the British Library

ISBN 0 7011 7808 6

Typeset by Deltatype Ltd, Birkenhead, Merseyside
Printed and bound in Great Britain by
Mackays of Chatham, PLC

CONTENTS

Rudderless, like driftwood I have run with the tides
While a grey-green ooze seeped through my leaking sides
And sluiced the planks . . . What did I long for if not to make
  amends,
The rock-pool's slop of brine, the sandcastle's brackish moat,
The pond where an unhappy child launched his little boat?
— Too late, all the dead in the river are my friends.

COUSINS

A Sunday at home, since I still called them that,
The house, the garden and the patch of lawn in front
Long gone to weeds and waist-high grasses
That I crawled round, hacking wildly with the shears
He'd once wielded – thick with rust now, blunt
And useless. I sweated under his old battered hat
While she poked at flowerbeds or sat
Marooned in a deckchair and wiped her glasses
That had misted with her hot flush, or with tears . . .

Then, after I had followed her indoors
For a 'sit-down' and a cup of tea, a 'chat',
I drifted from room to room and idly opened drawers;
With thumb-stained packs of cards, a pen that leaked
And corkscrews from Africa, I found
A locket that held two faded comma-curls
Of the hair 'they were famous for', two girls
In blackened-silver frames, pretty, cherub-cheeked;
With them, a stack of letters, brittle, browned,

In your great loss . . . such loveliness, beyond compare . . .
All innocent smiles, these sepia-tinted twins
Were her cousins twice-removed, long-dead –
Two angels, taken from us, one letter said,
That we might love them the more; and had they since
Stood in for all the losses she could neither share
Nor bear? To what had they been born? –
White dresses whispering over the croquet lawn,
Sun-blinds in the high-street, whiskery chaps

I

Who offered tigerish blazer-arms, the mill,
Tall masts at the ends of lanes, and blood-red maps? –
Men were employed to keep the Empire going
In distant, dark-skinned places, names no-one had heard
Till then, where light was like a great gong ringing
In the heavens, day after day, and where
The sun was not allowed to set. It was God's will,
Like the deaths they bloomed to, leeches clinging
Round their heads in place of clouds of hair.

I put them back and went out to the garden – there
The honeysuckle dripped, and dew-drops hung,
Convex mirrors in which I saw glowing
All that I'd been promised, if I could only wait
And work for it, the rewards of not dying young –
Suburban arcady, a deckchair and a blackbird
Perched in the branches of laburnum, singing –
And all of it would end with her, and wouldn't care.
'Come on, dear, come back in. It's getting late.'

TALES OF THE RIVERBANK

The Beaulieu river. The Hamble. The yacht *Spray*
pointing up into Southampton Water,

skippered by my grandfather, with a crew of three –
his son-in-law, his grandson and his daughter.

My father and mother and me. Or is it Richmond, Kew,
the tidal stretch below Teddington? Wherever.

Leaf-crowded banks, my childhood crouched in the bows
as they dipped and slipped towards the sea, and the river

was lost and found, lost and found, endlessly . . .
At forty-five, unsound of limb, incompetent to crew

I cast off our moorings in a chandler's yard,
horizontal rain slanting over Buckler's Hard,

and steered due south in search of their old house,
of what had gone with childhood and *Let us pray* . . .

      ~

What has gone with *Spray*, their house and every other –
the skipper, half the crew, and all they thought to own

leaving me to walk the towpath, overgrown
with slimy weeds that almost claimed my mother

when I was four, and could not have caught her,
where I saw her slip-slide, almost, into the river

with an awkward wave and disappear underwater . . .

After forty years I might put away my fear,
I might be able to reclaim her and forgive her

and let it all go, throw back the green–red–gold perch
I caught for her, I had no other way to show I loved her,

that faded like the regimental flag in church
and the Red Ensign in my father's room – a 'souvenir' . . .

In bowler hat and sea–boots, the ferryman waits at the pier.

~

To walk through branch-tangle, green gloom, into the open,
the sky a cloudless azure, the sunlight rich-pulsing;

depths of dazzle, hill-slopes green with vines, and, gliding
through-under everything, delightful, the river.

No sedges sunk in mud diffuse their stink upon
your banks; to the water's edge the paths all wander

safe from floods. In your shallows, limpid, slow-moving,
weeds and water-grasses tremble, while the furrowed

sand is shaken by a sudden gust, and shivered
to a thousand glints the choppy surface; pebbles,

gravel frame the green mosses, where the grayling
and the glistening roach, the chub, the whiskered barbel

and the gudgeon all slide slant-wise against the current.
What river-hues, when evening drives the lazy shadows . . .

~

We fished in waterlight, in greenish-brown
mud–redolence at evening, water lapping

at the bank where I sit now, where I never saw
those two walk together, as they did before

4

I was born; or, how they were before the war
broke him and her father's death broke her, her stare

cold and frightened from the other shore
he could not set out for from his whisky-chair,

turning through some farther circle of despair . . .

The bank by which I now set so much store,
where I caught the perch I left overnight in its glair,

that poisoned everything, poisoned the very air —
the bank where I have come to dream or drown . . .

A fish jumps, with the sound of its Creator clapping.

～

What he would have given . . . What he gave,
so I could leave behind his south London suburbs

and the river's sweetish, rank, mud-redolent air
for true South, his favourite jellied eels ('the best')

for sea-bass or salmon 'and its herbs',
his pub-poured whisky for the village square

and a local wine. His life no-one could save
for mine. Now I would give him back with interest

the years of work, of worrying over money, so that he
might point her slender bow into this wave —

Galatea, the sloop he did not live to see —
I want it all for him, who wanted it for me.

And *Spray* is gone, and so are all of them, and I
am their memory, and they must not altogether die.

THE CLASSICAL PICNIC

To pass through an arched gate and a shady arbour
From the Terrace garden
And its sternly ordered rose-beds, barbered lawns – barely
A distance of two paces –
Was to enter a different world entirely.
My arm around her waist would guide her
Towards a riot of nettles, buttercups, wild grasses:
After the narrow straits of deckchairs
It felt like coming into harbour.
We knew it only as The Meadow,
Though it had other names among the locals,
Distressed gentlefolk and old-age pensioners
Who gazed at lily-ponds and fountains from their benches.
Our loitering steps slowed to a standstill
And then we'd sink together in some shadow.
Inevitably, she'd help everything to harden
And I'd slide one finger, two, inside her.

Thistles grew there, and midges in cloud-clusters
Swarmed to us, and we were sometimes flustered
By the proximity of other couples
Who found the same use for the place as we did,
Oblivious to that snake in the grass, the river
As it glinted away into the valley;
Some walked their dogs there, and the odd voyeur
Prowled around until he got an eyeful.
What did it matter, as long as we could lie together?
And once, believing in our carnal innocence
That all this hot fumbling made us grown-ups,
We decided to act as grown-ups seemed to,
Pretending that the pleasure we knew awaited us
Was not the purpose of our outing,
And took food and drink, which we spread on a blanket –

There's even garlands for you, violet wreaths and saffron,
And lilies plucked where they grow by the virgin river,
And little cheeses that they dry in baskets of rushes,
And plums that ripen in the autumn weather,
And chestnuts, and the cheerful red of apples.
In brief, here's Ceres, love, and rowdy Bacchus —
And red-stained blackberries, and grapes in bunches,
And hanging from his frame, sea-green cucumber.
And here's the little god who keeps the arbour,
Fierce with his sickle and enormous belly. —
You be damned, you with your Puritan eyebrows!
What thanks will cold ashes give for the sweetness of garlands?
Or do you intend to hang a rose-wreath on your tombstone?
Set down the wine and the dice and perish who thinks of tomorrow!
Here's death twitching my ear: 'Live', says he, 'for I'm coming'.

PROSE

We knew we'd never had it so good
when Ted Heath sailed away on *Morning Cloud*.

Power-cuts and the three-day week.
A country held to ransom by the miners' strike.

While my father sat dozing in his favourite Parker-Knoll
my mother carried on with one and all

and I went deeper into felt life, wrecked my eyesight
reading *Lady Chatterley* by candlelight.

ALBUM

Unmoving on the mock-Tudor sideboard
lived those interesting strangers,
my relatives: among hollyhocks and hydrangeas

they grinned their sepia grins for ever
and went on with lives of deckchair-endeavour
in spite of war or failure, drink, the locked ward . . .

They hadn't made it as my father had
out of the world of red-brick villas,
laurel and laburnum and a bandstand playing
'Pomp and Circumstance' when he was a boy;

they hadn't travelled like *his* dad
or my mother's, beyond the stuccoed pillars
and the bamboo tables and the fraying
palms. Fought shy of *hoi polloi*.

∼

Two black sheep, disguised in pith hats
and khaki tunics, looking grand
against a background of the ghats
and grouped around a handsome sikh —

Jim and Cecil, before they came
back home to smirch the family name
and piss the family fortune away.

Their riding-boots still wink and shine,
their backs are stiff, a hand
rests on a shoulder, and the pencil-line

beneath each face's floating camouflage
of ponderous moustaches seems to bespeak
the unspoken rightness of the Raj.
Oh yes, they had their day.

∽

There he is on the whitewashed veranda,
beside a flowering jacaranda
and his daughter and his daughter's ayah;

a big man in Malaya,
portly, in his white linen suit
and puffing on a thin cheroot,
he looks over grove on grove of rubber.

At fifty, he has lost two homes, his hair
and his first yacht; a second rides the swell
at Bursledon. He has a son as well
but his years as manager-landlubber

will end when that white smoke in the air
becomes the ghost-blur on his young wife's lung.
My mother's mother. Twenty-eight years young.

∽

Uncle Basil! Basil Gascoigne, not quite
Ealing comedy in spite
of his name, his loud ties, sporting checks
and waistcoat watch-chain; flecks

of baccy in his George V full set;
his young man's wooden tennis racquets
and endless Player's Navy packets –
'I'm *dying* for a cigarette!'

We all laughed, Uncle, but you were.
And here's Eileen, high heels and fur,
a waft of scent, of G&T.

Married wrong, unable to divorce,
you 'lived in sin' and steered your glamorous course
through bars and racetracks to the sea . . .

~

And that west-country fishing-port
where he stands for ever on a slipway –
behind him are the sloops and ketches
rocking gently in their own

reflections, and a boat-house roof
sloping gently, as in one of his early sketches;
the sea to him is beauty, it is sport

but he will not now ever own
a sloop, a ketch, a dinghy even, while
he has watched so often with a smile
so many tides come in and slip away

and leave him high and dry, that only 60 proof
can float him off; there he'll stand
for good, my father, smiling, tanned.

GALATEA

When you left, and I was thinner-skinned
I stayed in bed for weeks and cried and cried . . .
Where rigging whined and rattled in the wind
I scrunched alone through broken bottles, claws,
The bleached brittle crusts of starfish, crab –
A salt-rich tide of little deaths – and I could hear,
In that click–click of pebbles when the sea withdraws
Her high heels on the pavement. *That was the end of us . . .*
Back down 'on business', I take a bus
Past the shut–down shop–fronts and collapsing pier
To the beach, the little café where I wrote

(So long ago!) 'through wood and weeds, washed up
Like bottles, torn shoes and a plastic cup
We walked without a word, and parted', and I choke
On the smells of vinegar, and steam, and smoke –
Outside, a salt drizzle blurs the shelves
Where the clattering hiss of shingle meets the sigh
And roar of water, where on hot days we used to lie
Like sea–creatures on the sea–bed, their ultrasound
Antennae groping, or the fish we saw
Laid glistening on the fishmonger's slab
But could not afford to eat – how we starved ourselves

For love, learning, poetry! How ill-informed
And unreasonable we were, how raw!
Is she waiting for me, on the scrubby bit of ground
Where I got her to agree the thing had died
And she ran off, crying, in the rain –
Staring as she used to when she lay awake
And listened to that squat colossus, watched it rake
Our bedroom with its cyclops eye? A giant claw
Gouged up the sea-floor, dug up the drowned;
A generator throbbed like a migraine,
In the harbour, tugs and dredgers swarmed . . .

Or at the Metropole, twice married,
Reading *Persuasion* over tea, her smile remote,
Benign? No, she is spindrift, carried
On the wind, the voice of one ill wind or another
That blows me and my leaking boat no good –
Whenever you go out, in your little craft of wood,
Your little craft of words, it will be me you hear,
It will be me reminding you of how you scorned your mother
And all women who loved you (God knows why),
It will be me reminding you that you will die,
It will be me reminding you of everything you fear.

Wildlife

She loved the mountain ash that flowered above the garden,
outside my bedroom window – the tiny four-square garden
that they weeded, tended, watered through my childhood
after lunch on Sundays, trimming privet, planting wallflowers;
then one year I came home and the patch of garden
had grown smaller, meaner, it had shrunk like childhood,
the fence and privet hedge were gone, and there instead
was a little low wall behind which the wallflowers
and mountain ash looked foolish . . . The bright seed-packs of
   childhood
are gone now, there are brochures for old people's homes,
the mountain ash has gone too, the stump is dead
and 'Next Spring I'll see about the garden', I say mildly
to the old woman who lives here, a widow, and the fox that
   roams
through waist-high grasses as she watches from the window,
   staring wildly.

Tidal

These winding streets are *liable to sudden flooding*
and now I glimpse the river through leaves of oak and beech
and horse-chestnut, my eyes are liable to sudden flooding
as I think of how he courted her along this green suburban
    reach
in the leaf-rich summers, in the bonfire-scented autumns
on the Surrey side, in the suburbs of his pleasure
before he was allotted (and he knew this was his portion)
other men's allotments, squares of laurel and horse-chestnut,
avenues of limes; flotsam-scattered cobbled slipways,
houseboats, boathouses, the smell of mud on slipways
when the tide has flooded them, towpaths shaded by horse-
    chestnut
where they walked together, a sense of due proportion
in all things, in their pain as in their pleasure,
in the river-borne summers of their life, and the smoky
    autumns.

Artistes

The scents of lavender and lilac bring back my grandmother
for all the world as if she had just come through the doorway
from the garden, its sunblind bleached by fifty summers
into the room with lacquered cabinets and dried rose-petals
in a big bowl on the piano, holding a spray of lilac
and a sprig of lavender – the lilac she would stand in vases
that trembled slightly when she attacked the piano
fortissimo, and waved away the smiles of all-comers
with her handkerchief that still smells of lavender
as my sister glimmers by on points towards the doorway
beyond which stand the lilac, waiting for its vases,
and the pear and plum trees in the garden and hours at the
    piano
among black lacquered cabinets and chintz-covered settles
and with her goes the ballet-dancing girlhood of my
    grandmother.

ROTISSERIE (THE WAIT)

*'There's a feeling of disaster in the air, which I now know I have felt
  for a long time.'* Ian Hamilton, May 2001

Our usual place, and everything in it
Exactly as we had learned to expect:
Most tables empty, the 'interfered-with air'
Heavy with the stink of re-cooked fat
That got into the clothes, into the hair
Along with cigarettes smoked at such a rate
It was like a race, and you had to win it;

The 'maître d'', a supercilious queer
Who knew we had too much class to be there
(These nights, I have to keep going back
To meet you, though it's still only me there) . . .
Breathless from the cold, my coat unchecked
I found our usual table, where I sat;
'Some wine, *sir*?' 'No thanks', I said, 'I'll wait.'

And wait I did, my *Standard* open at
The horoscopes (Predictions for New Year!
Your Stars, That Break, and You! – as if),
My mind snagged on Failure of Drug Czar,
My eye swivelling from page to watch
And back again, and then to some
Embarrassing art-work above the bar . . .

Once or twice, I'd known you to be late
But there'd never been a time you hadn't come,
Grim-faced, apologizing. So I sat on,
Through the looks of waitresses who guessed
I'd been stood up, who wondered what had gone
So wrong for me I'd choose this place for a date;
Through the 'chef's' indifference, the whiff

Of something raw, the turning spit. It was a test,
A trial of sorts. And since what we are
Takes the piss out of what we wish we were
And nothing we can do helps shake off 'the dread
That how we live measures our own nature'
(How many times had you quoted *that*?),
I ordered, first a scotch, and then another scotch.

The room forgot me. I didn't have to stir.
Any moment, you'd come in, take off the hat
You wore to hide the fluff of white hair growing back
Now you were 'in remission' – from the drugs –
And sit down, drink and smoke. (You never ate;
Just pushed things round and round your plate
Till you could decently light up again.)

A couple slouched in, a few single men
And glancing round each time I heard the door
I logged a face or two, flushed from the street,
For when you turned up, as you would any minute;
Would you 'just have to go and make a call'?
Or, patting pockets for reserves of ten
And feigning interest in the menu, greet

Our waitress with a show of blinks and shrugs? –
Such gentle flirting . . . Christ, that was months ago.
No jokes, now, about the new kid on the 'scene',
Your last advance, or what you had to do before
You could be let off, the slate wiped clean . . .
As if. Were you trying to get through?
Or slumped in a cab – another scare?

I dialled your number, spoke to your machine;
Then sat again. Did I '*want* anything at all?' –
No thanks, I said, and went on with the wait, not knowing
(And how like you, somehow, that I should not know)
What strange new circumstance prevented you
From joining me, from getting up and going,
To the phone, out to the tall night, anywhere.

EFFECTS

I held her hand, that was always scarred
From chopping, slicing, from the knives that lay in wait
In bowls of washing-up, that was raw,
The knuckles reddened, rough from scrubbing hard
At saucepan, frying pan, cup and plate
And giving love the only way she knew,
In each cheap cut of meat, in roast and stew,
Old-fashioned food she cooked and we ate;
And I saw that they had taken off her rings,
The rings she'd kept once in her dressing-table drawer
With faded snapshots, long-forgotten things
(Scent-sprays, tortoise-shell combs, a snap or two
From the time we took a holiday 'abroad')
But lately had never been without, as if
She wanted everyone to know she was his wife
Only now that he was dead. And her watch? –
Classic ladies' model, gold strap – it was gone,
And I'd never known her not have *that* on,
Not in all the years they sat together
Watching soaps and game shows I'd disdain
And not when my turn came to cook for her,
Chops or chicken portions, English, bland,
Familiar flavours she said she preferred
To whatever 'funny foreign stuff'
Young people seemed to eat these days, she'd heard;
Not all the weeks I didn't come, when she sat
Night after night and stared unseeing at
The television, at her inner weather,
Heaved herself upright, blinked and poured
Drink after drink, and gulped and stared – the scotch
That, when he was alive, she wouldn't touch,
That was her way to be with him again;
Not later in the psychiatric ward,
Where she blinked unseeing at the wall, the nurses
(Who would steal anything, she said), and dreamt
Of when she was a girl, of the time before

I was born, or grew up and learned contempt,
While the TV in the corner blared
To drown some 'poor soul's' moans and curses,
And she took her pills and blinked and stared
As the others shuffled round, and drooled, and swore . . .
But now she lay here, a thick rubber band
With her name on it in smudged black ink was all she wore
On the hand I held, a blotched and crinkled hand
Whose fingers couldn't clasp mine any more
Or falteringly wave, or fumble at my sleeve –
The last words she had said were *Please don't leave*
But of course I left; now I was back, though she
Could not know that, or turn her face to see
A nurse bring the little bag of her effects to me.

VISIT

'The evenings are drawing in', she said,
Turning her matted-silver, wispy head
To the window from her hospital bed,

And it brought back an afternoon
When she'd said it once before, in June,
And I knew I would be losing her soon.

But this time it was true; the days
Were shorter, though she fixed her gaze
On something that, for all our ways

Of being close, I could not see:
Beyond the darkening branch, the tree
Obliterated finally,

The expected moment that would bring
Not nurse, or son, or anything
To make her better, help her cling

For one short day more
But violence that would shake her to the core
And end the dance of shadows on the floor.

Pain too. Though she could not admit
Her longing to be out of it –
Her whole life one long bout of it –

That hour would also bring release
To one who'd known so little peace;
Not since I was born, at least,

That other June which was, she said,
The last time she had turned her head
To the window from a hospital bed.

New leaves, then, on that same tree, new life
Surrounding her, a still-young wife
And mother. No surgeon's knife

Had probed where she was swollen, cut
And pried apart her flesh, tight-shut,
No fingers prodded her distended gut

Or, more shocking, latex-sheathed,
Penetrated 'down there' while she breathed
The hot air, disinfectant-wreathed

And felt how she was pregnant with
A living thing that meant her death,
Not those cells that gave me breath,

Not a thing of pride and joy for her –
A barrel-chested baby boy for her –
But strength no bottle could destroy for her,

Gross, unmentionable, a clot
Of griefs that grew to what she'd 'got' . . .
Did she know, as I did not,

That she would sprout a dried-blood beard
The night that it appeared? –
The end of fear, and what she feared.

THREE-PIECE SUITE

The battered leather sofa that spilled horse-hair,
that I knocked the stuffing out of, a stiff coarse hair
like wires – my crippled tank, B-17 or Lanc
limping home on a wing and a prayer;

the bamboo table where, in a previous life, she'd taken
tea in the whitewashed, sepia-tinted shade,
that now, Sunday tea-times, was visibly shaken
by whatever cake she'd made;

the painted screen that shielded, once, her mother's bed,
that showed all the richness that had been Malaya's,
humming-birds, Japonica, a rubber-tree,
the loss of which had left a small persistent ache . . .

Her clutching one or other of the three
in the middle of cleaning, wincing, murmuring 'My *head* . . .',
her singing, *Bali Ha'i, I hear you calling*
from the depths . . . Come to me, come to me;

her defeated air, her telling me to take
from the round tobacco-scented tin of fifty Players
two bright white cigarettes – no filter tips –
to tip the coalman, Jeffries – no first names –

who waited at the back door with his empty sacks
and his rich, mysterious smell, his bright white grin
as he mimed bringing a cigarette to his lips;
her grandmother falling, falling

in the night, and the blood, and no-one
ever speaking of it, and the grim determination
with which I delivered 'coal' – my father's paperbacks –
and waited for it all to go up in flames.

~

They were married in the winter of '47,
a bad one but for her who wilted in the heat
a blessing, frost-starred. The year of *South Pacific*,
of 'Some Enchanted Evening', 'Bali Ha'i' . . .

Ten years of rationed happiness. The Christmas, '54
end-of-term concert at her father's school in Devon
she sang the aria from *Madame Butterfly*;
curled pink pupa that would soon start to make her sick,

I slept through it; my sister sat with the score
in her gingham lap, jaw dropping as our mother twirled
a rice-paper parasol and hit the highest note . . .
Later, Mummy's little man, I trailed after her

lugging her father's huge ex-Navy coat
on my skinny shoulders, I was the busman, I shouted 'Fares'
while she heaped up coals to warm their three
unheated rooms, their three-piece suite –

I was rewarded by indulgent grown-up laughter,
loose change chinking, 'One please';
as she swept a duster over tables, flicked at chairs
she sang *Some enchanted evening, you may see a stranger*

or 'Un bel di vedremo' (just the tune)
and dreamt of evenings on the South Pacific or the China seas,
or remembered times she'd partnered him in the skating pairs
but found the noise and crowds too much,

or was a girl in that other world,
rubber-trees, the sudden rustle of monsoon . . .
But when had she met the man who stood in our door,
who spoke American to her, who wore

a trenchcoat that made him look like Gregory Peck
or was it Tyrone Power, who came in 'for a cup of tea'
and stayed for hours, talking softly, who moved to touch
her hand? All the years she was at the 'beck

and call' of that same granny dear
who would so easily bring her to her knees,
growing madder, meaner, dog-in-the-manger,
and I never thought of how her head swam, how it swirled

on Richmond Hill, not from vertigo for once but to see come
    clear
those blade-etched frost-shapes on the ice-rink,
whorls and stars, her head always teetering on the brink;
or of how a life could go, could shrivel-shrink

to one overheated room, a stained armchair,
a cheap transistor and a handful of tapes, among them
no *Madame Butterfly* or *South Pacific*, and a glare
of surprised fear when I reminded her she'd sung them.

&

It was *Madame Butterfly* as she went into the fire,
it was Maria Callas singing 'Un bel di
vedremo', not a dry eye in the house, her eyes
had melted, and all the flesh that had been her,

and the black, bitter growths she'd almost heaved
from her bloated body, all went to ash, to the air
as Callas sang her favourite aria and we grieved
silently, my sister's face crumpling as she hit top C;

her hair that had gone at last to grey, her hair,
her poor bent bones, all went to smoke that curled
from the crematorium chimney – a carefully-timed
half-hour was all it took; and I thought of how I was free,

of Tyrone Power and Gregory Peck, her father,
mine, and I tried to swallow back the sighs
that shook me, gulps and sighs, and Callas climbed
the scale of grief and longing, higher, higher.

LAUNDERETTE: HER LAST NIGHTDRESS

A cotton one with a few flowers and a bit of lace
At the neck, her name-tag stitched inside, it falls
From my bag of socks and shirts and smalls
And looks so innocent, so out of place
I see her again, hot and flustered in the ward

We took her to, and helpless, late at night
When even she admitted 'something wasn't right'
And I left her waving, and she sort of smiled
To say I mustn't worry, must get on,
Get back, to sleep, to work, to my important life.

Next day, I went to M&S, I bought
The nightdress she had asked for as an afterthought
And took it in to her, and she put it on
And loved it – no more the sad, unreconciled,
Bewildered woman I had fought, no more

My father's tetchy, disappointed wife;
Girlish, almost. So it was what she wore
Until one day I walked in and found her lying
In a hospital gown, so starched and plain
And straitlaced, with strings that needed tying

While this pretty one had gone into her drawer –
The something that was wrong had made a stain,
A stench I took away with me somehow
To wash, and forgot about till now
I stand here in the warm soap-smelling air

But can't remember why, and people stare.

ORPHEUS

What is life to me without thee?
                                  Much the same,
except that I can't hear the great aria
sung by Kathleen Ferrier
and not be filled with longing and with shame,
so uncannily her portrait on the CD cover
resembles you; so uncannily her 1950s perm
brings you back to me, that first day of term,
waving me on to school. I missed you like a lover
and would have clawed through concrete and earth
to be at home with you, who had to let me go,
who gave me such a sense of my own worth
that I sing with her, as if Orpheus was my name . . .

                    ～

What is left if thou art dead?
                                  My attic flat,
the cat you took such pleasure in, who wonders why
I sit so late, and drink, and do not go to bed
to sleep an hour or so then wake
and soak the clammy pillow for your sake,
who comforts me with purring in her sleep,
the gentle sleep she offers like a gift;
who does not as I do turn over in her head
the knowledge that you died between the night and morning
    shift,
that as you felt yourself slip
you heaved up the black bitter years that would dry
on your cold dead lips; she does not know that.

                    ～

Thy dear lord am I so faithful?
                              No more or less
than when I bundled you into a wheelchair
in a stained pink hospital quilt
and the dazed smiles of women stranded in the regimen
of sleep and pills, your new friends, were rooting for us
as we struggled to that suburban high street where
you sat for your last wash and perm;
and we came back to their wondering chorus
of 'Ooh, lovely, dear', and you were young again,
touching your new hair, and I was without guilt
and loved you as on that first day of term,
as if I had won you back by this huge success.

FADO

How all things cohere, some days, how all things conspire –
if I had not been walking past the window of a sushi bar
in Soho just as the sunset caught it in a flash of fire
I would not have noticed its backdrop flag of Japan,
would not have thought of her, of that song (*Wherever you are,
it's 3 a.m.*) or of the time she died, she was so embarrassed,
thirteen, walking the aisle of the airbus in her best white
harem-pants, realising that a patch of red
had begun to seep, to seep and darken and spread
and she had to walk the length of that aisle to find her seat
and reach to stow a bag before she could sit and hide her
    shame;
or of the photograph I took of her lying bare-assed
on my bed, waving me away with one hand that holds
a cigarette in fingers that are daubed and dabbled red;
would not have noticed how the sunset drained and bled
into itself, how it drained itself of purples, golds
and crimsons to become a dull rust-red-brown (the same
rust-red-brown as radiator-water, as blood washed out of a
    sheet);
would not have thought of her driving all day in the heat
to a hill-town in Portugal, a cellar bar, those two Japanese
who laughed all through the fado-singer's guttural sobs . . .
Of how I lay unmoving in the dark beneath the fan
in our hotel room while she came and went, all night,
came and went, would not have thought of those gobbets and
    gobs
of red that drained down the bowl from which, bent
almost double, she looked at me, finally, on my knees;
of that song, *How did it ever come so far . . .*

HERITAGE

England, and a drive through farms,
through dripping lanes, bumper-deep in mud,
diseased herds suffering the weather
and pubs where couples drained their years together,
sitting with pursed lips and crossed arms
over pints of bitter and tomato juice,
and me chewing my own bitter cud,
and me logging all of it for future use

in some piece of versified revenge
as we joined the tailback past Stonehenge
and Salisbury, past Keep Out signs
and mile on mile of razor-wire,
past the prehistoric mines
and dug-outs, fox-holes, shelling-scars,
past the skyward-pointing spire
and mile on mile of oncoming cars;

just to drift through panelled rooms, past walls
of flushed, same-featured faces
or wander round some flowering oasis
while I, stiff from the drive down, bored
half to death, hung-over, sour with guilt
imagined my hard-earned reward:
her cupped hand on my tightened balls,
her legs parting slyly under the B&B's damp quilt . . .

≁

The paths we trudged through Somethingshire!
And once she said, out of the blue
if we couldn't talk, if all we could share
was time, there wasn't any point in going on –
bad enough, but the bigger scare
(this stopped me in my tracks, it's true)
was waiting by the twisted tree
I ducked behind to answer – as did she –

that 'call of nature' (from the beer):
a cow's skull, grinning. *Soon you will be gone,*
it said; *what can you share but this,*
but time, your moment here? Which will pass,
as fleeting as the pause before a wave,
as your footsteps on this grass
which might be covering your grave.
Caught short, you are nothing, piss

and wind, a shrunken cock, the Kleenex-scrap
she wipes herself with, that is whipped into the void —
as you will be. (She hoiked up her pants,
I mimed absorption in some guidebook crap ...)
This is no myth, no chivalric romance:
you won't sit for ever in the dappled shade
of oak and beech, such as you once enjoyed;
you won't be reborn, you'll dwindle, fade

and disappear, become your names
illegible on a lichen-covered headstone
in some forgotten churchyard, overgrown
with weeds and briars and brambles
or go to ash, to smoke and air
inbreathed by nature-lovers on their rambles —
who will watch you slide into the flames
and shed a shy, a shuddering tear?

No silent gratitude in Georgian rooms
(Family Solicitors, Commissioners for Oaths),
no deeds of trust, no much-loved homes,
no legacy of life, no precious heirlooms —
what good are they without a sodding heir? —
just a few hundred well-thumbed 'tomes',
a thrift-shop rack of stale-smelling clothes,
some letters tied with ribbon, 'Dear —' ...

~

Breakfast: while she watched her eggs congeal
I contemplated circumcised remains
of sausage, and a bacon-rind;
an hour before, I'd fucked her from behind
and now her face wore all the strain
of wanting not to punish me,
of battling indecisively
some hurt of mine she could not heal . . .

Back, then, through half-timbered towns,
past the homes of billionaires
who long ago cashed in their shares
and bought England, whose slim blonde wives
work out and punish four-wheel-drives
on their way to an assignation
over lunch in the hotel lounge, 'The Downs';
past the theme-park (Heritage Nation)

where the beer-bellies, shaven heads
and shiny shell-suits swarm
over litter-strewn lawns, and storm
the Bouncy Castle and the potting sheds
'Now selling lager, lolly's, video's';
past the lane that every flasher knows;
past the woods where little girls take root.
And none of this would bear fruit.

THE FIREBREAK

A slow hot firebreak through the burning bush (by Arthur
   Boyd)
and the old tyre up ahead, dead-centre of it, dusty-black,
that made a gentle bump as we drove right over it

was a coiled sleeping snake. I shouted *Stop the car. Go back!*
and knelt down and touched the scaly head we'd split,
that was my own two minds for the next few miles;

whatever broken, oozing thing was on *her* mind
she drove in silence and then stopped again, all smiles
and said *Come on, forget it* but I heard the electric hum

of the crickets' disapproval and the kookaburras' laughter
and, high up in the branches of a scribbled-on scribbly gum,
I saw that snake, watching. It opened wide its jaw and hissed

Either you're suffering from the heat or you've been pissed
once too often, mate. What's got into you? Don't come
the raw prawn with me. A real bloke, having scored a blonde

would cart her off with him to the outback of beyond,
not write sestinas on her arse. Life's a bitch and death comes after.
What are you waiting for? With no children, it's just void.

And then she started up the car and they were far behind,
the firebreak and the forest, and in the place of fear
came a new freedom and loneliness. In the clear.

THE LOVE OF UNKNOWN WOMEN

Young women with damp hollows, downy arms,
Bare burnished legs – you see them striding
Towards their plant-filled offices, riding
Bicycles to flatshares after work; lunchtimes, you stare
As secretaries, backpackers tanned from birth
Peel off their things and stretch on sun-warmed earth.

A few of them stare back . . . As if they'd share
Their world of holidays and weekend farms
With you! – They step more lightly every year,
A glimpse of neck-hair, a scent that lingers, girls
Who, swinging bags with shops' names, disappear,
Trailing glances, into crowds; each one unfurls

Her special beauty like a fragile frond
Before your famished eyes. *I am what lies beyond,*
They seem to say, *beyond the mortgage, car and wife –*
I am what you deserve, I am the buried life
You will never live. Are they pushed laughing on to beds
By hands that unhook bras and yank down briefs?

Do they wake with tongues furred, heads
Hot and unremembering? Crave purls
Of water, cool as their long fingers? Schubert, jazz,
It's all the same to them. As are your little griefs.
It isn't fair. If you've not changed, what has?
Is it a kind of shifting, imperceptible, like sands

On some barren, windswept stretch of shore?
In simmering parks, on summer streets
You think of her, and furtively explore
The curves of eyebrow, cheek and lip –
Of other things too; you search left hands
For seals of love, or ownership. They smell your old defeats.

OUT OF SEASON

The furniture shone with a wax-polished gleam
In the bright little bar where we lingered over whisky.
Voices were low, it was warm and *intime*.
Outside, some chairs shivered in a wind off the sea.

EPITHALAMIUM

It is the last official day of summer;
In this medieval-Roman market town
Of sewer-smells in narrow streets, become a
Place of pilgrimage, of ritual stopping-off
For those who've 'always had a thing about Van Gogh',
I choose a café-table and sit down –
A view of ochre roofs, a plain, a mountain,
Half-rock, half-haze; a lion-headed fountain
And a statue of the local genius, hotels
In pastel colours, fruit stalls, oyster shells.

And think of what it was that brought me here:
Translating verses by a man whose name
Was writ on Vichy water, who splashed more per year
In tips to valets, coachmen, waiters, clerks
Than I'll earn from a lifetime's 'literary works',
My not-yet-wearied-of mug's game:
Valery Larbaud. He lived to travel, and to write;
Did he, I wonder, come back night after night
To the pool of lamplight on his desk? Prefer
Le blanc vierge du papier to her,

Or her? (He liked them young, and virginal.)
Did he hell. *The rich are different.* But why
Should this *riche amateur* have had it all?
I've praised his work in print, now I'll come clean
About my envy (I would call it *spleen*
If opium and clap were standing by) . . .
Yet I've no cause to envy anyone, in fact:
At forty-something, more or less intact
In mind and body, I've a roof, a bed
And cash, I'm well-watered and well-fed;

One of the lucky ones, I've reached my 'prime'.
It isn't such an awful place to be,
With friends and books and booze to pass the time –

So, no whingeing in ungrateful tones
About the fees X earns, the things Y owns.
If Larbaud's Europe ever was reality –
His polished Pullman cars, his varnished yachts –
It isn't now, and wasn't for have-nots.
The planet's fucked; but that's been on the cards
Since someone struck a spark from stony shards . . .

A roar of mopeds fills the cobbled square
And blaring car-horns startle every street;
Swifts and martins seek the safety of the air,
Shutters creak as ageing eyes peer out
From darkly-furnished rooms to see what it's about,
Pernod-sippers rise in one wave to their feet.
On confetti-strewn church steps they stand,
Awkward, reddened, grinning, hand in hand,
He stiff in his one suit, she a froth of lace
Who have just chosen – what? One voice, one face

From all the voices, faces, that are now
The past, and irrecoverably sealed –
By that odd business with a ring, a vow –
In separate jars just big enough to hold
Their twenty years; chosen to grow old
Using up on children all their lives might yield.
Or is *that* where I'd really like to be?
The waiter, when I call for *encore un demi*
Mutters something to himself, and smirks;
With my notebook, pen and Larbaud's Works

In front of me, I'm not fooling anyone,
Is what he means, and my French-friendly air
Can't hide the fact that I'm here on the run,
Weighed down by baggage that I've always carried,
Unappeased, unsettled and unmarried
After yet another almost-love affair;
Losing ground to that pub-haunter, rank
With my last whisky, last bad dream, last wank,

A slack-mouthed bore who waits until I'm pissed
To tell me, slurring – but I get the gist –

How all of this will end, how all will fade
Along with my own scribbles, out of print,
How the chances missed, the friends betrayed,
The love I did not want or could not keep
Will be there always and will not let me sleep,
How absolutely no-one . . . Not a hint . . .
The same voice, too familiar, and crude
In its insinuations, phlegm-soaked, stewed,
Wonders why I'm skulking here instead
Of trying to repair those things I said –

Unless I really want to be alone
For ever, and pretend that that's okay
And stick with what I know, have always known
As if I was *some buffer born in twenty-five*
Who acts like he was only half-alive . . .
Or could I find a girl here? Set up, stay? –
Those two climb in a car and clatter through
A town that stops to make their choice seem true
And right and real; and I am at a loss
To know why some hearts meet, while others only cross.

I'm not at home, and trying to be French
By ordering a dish of *tripes* in wine
I merely feel more sharply what a wrench
It would be to leave all that behind – my life,
My single room, my no-child-no-wife-
And-no-regrets; but *Larbaud's* life, not mine,
Is what I want – or think I want – again. . . .
No answers here. Soon I'll be on a train
Heading back to what I know, what I must love,
The loneliness that fits me like a glove.

ROTISSERIE (THE RETURN)

And yes, it *was* a kind of stair I passed you on,
Or else some sort of escalator;
You smiled lopsidedly and doffed the hat
You wore *to hide that fluff of white hair growing back*
Now you were in remission – from the drugs –
But you were on your way up from your 'Mr Bleaney flat'
While I was on my way down here,
The turning spit, the stink of burning fat
That they would use and re-use and re-use
And the maître d', *a supercilious queer*
Who knew we had too much class
To be there – though I keep going back . . .

I found our usual table, where I sat.
Had you just gone to make a call?
Or buy reserves of ten?
I remembered your old lighter in my pocket –
In its metal casing, heavy as a gun;
They always came back in the end, you swore,
Having done the rounds. I tried to cock it
But it wouldn't spark, my thumb
Was rubber . . . Glancing round each time I heard the door
I logged a face or two for when
You came back – but you didn't come,
To feign an interest in the menu, fail to choose
And blind our waitress with a smile, a show of shrugs . . .

For once, I didn't know what to expect:
Was it a trial, a test of some kind, without booze?
Penance for something said or done?
Why no 'sizzling specials' chalked up on the slate?
Why that vinegary drizzle – electric organ,
Was it? ('You'll never walk alone'.) And whose
That coffin, 'scrubbed, magnificently decked',
Trundling towards the jets of flame?

It was too dark for me to read the name
On the beautifully-embossed brass plate.
Did I *want* anything at all?' –
No thanks, I said, my friend will be here soon.
Not true;
But I sat on, not knowing
What strange new circumstance prevented you
From sitting down with me, and three hours later
Knocking back a last glass
With stage-winces for the waiter,
Stubbing out the last Royal and going,
Home, out to the tall night, anywhere.

AS IF

The scents of cedar, maple and pitch-pine
through the open window brought her back,
I spun the car off US 101, the slightly curved spine
between Hopland and Cloverdale, no turning back
and climbed out and started clawing at the earth
with my bare hands, as if, as if
I might open wide its great cunt and it give birth,
as if I might get down to what was left,
the tattooes on her arms and back,
the scars of her breasts, the sour-sweet whiff
of her arse, of her cleft,
as if I might bring her back
by getting to grips again with what
was once gym-hardened muscle, now was not –

was now parchment skin and brittle bone –
and feel her twitching under me, feel her squirm,
as if I might anoint her parched mouth, her baked-earth back
with my tears and sperm
and lie and listen to the sigh and moan
of the wind as it scoured the grass
and whipped up silver on the sea's black back
and raised goose-bumps on her arse
and stirred the hairs at the base of her spine,
as if I could get to her, as if she could be mine
and I could fuck her on her back
and fuck her lying on her front,
could fuck her once more in the ass and in the cunt
until she came so much it brought her back;

as if she could kick-start and ride
her massive Harley with me behind, could ride
and have me like that, while she gripped the steering,
as if I could kneel above her back,
its whorls and swirls, a snake's head disappearing
in the valley of the shadow, could come to grips
with her cropped head and Navajo earring
and the rings in her lips,
her nether lips, could dunt that snake until she cried
Now you! Shoot it up my back!
and I, obedient as ever, spent and fell back
and lay beside her, scents of opium and kif
in the night air, our talk as if, as if
she had never left me, as if she had never died.

A RECONSIDERATION

Dawn-mist on the river;
fog soon obscured both banks,
damp chill and green water
from a thousand leaks
in my rotting plywood hull
sluiced the cockpit planks
as I made for midstream, the screw
and bows fighting some resistance
as if the Thames had thickened
to ice, and I was an icebreaker
butting a passage through
to white and empty distance,
strafed by a single gull . . .
Time ran out, the tide ran
out, the river quickened
and all around the boat
I saw them in their thousands,
bobbing belly up, mouths
working, pleading with me,
blowing forlorn farewell kisses;
the silver-white heaps on the mud
of both banks flopped until
their gills had stopped
and they were still,
the mud was covered
and the air sickened . . .

How had I made this happen?
Perhaps someone I'd left
alone, in the lurch . . .
But I'd always been
the one to feel bereft!
If only I had thrown
back that little perch,
along with the foul-hooked
roach and dace, the bream
and gudgeon – no,
this might be a dream
but these deaths were real,
and when I looked
all eyes were focused on
a 'little muddy reach'
where men in twos and threes,
dark-coated, stood around
the white blur of a corpse – a girl,
from the shape she made,
the tuft that shivered
slightly in the breeze,
stretched out for her photo-call,
a silver sheet behind her
and one of them hunched over
a tripod, an arc-light's glare
enough to blind her . . .

I put in at Eel Pie Island,
the old tea-room where
one hot Sunday afternoon
forty years before (two weeks?)
I had sent cups and saucers,
the whole table flying –
my father's red-faced,
small gestures of repair,
my mother almost crying –
this time the scent of a wall
of roses knocked me sideways,
I went to pick one for her –
but who? *She* was half a world
away from me, from 'Tideways',
and my mother who'd loved
roses was long gone to ash
beneath a rosebush
in my sister's garden . . .
To go on or back? The flood
would bring its slew
of days like this one, of regret
for things done or undone;
the ebb a swirl
of regret for all I would not do.
I would wait there,
for the tide to reconsider.

10.

The girls who went for me at 'poetry events',
who knew their Germaine Greer, who said
they grieved for Sylvia (and slandered Ted),
where are they now? Or the PRs with more sense
but no head for drink – ships that passed
out in the night? How almost-incredible
those scenes are (*they all went by so fast*) . . .
Somewhere it is written down, indelible:
the all-day papers and the plenary sessions,
the half-hidden looks and shy confessions
in the late-night bar (those British Council jaunts
to Prague or Peshawar); her favourite haunts,
then in the taxi back to my hotel . . .
'Do you like Neruda?' 'Who doesn't?' (Do I hell.)

11.

The *fin de siècle*! Nostradamus, self-doubt!
Seized on a street corner by the Absolute
I readjust my tie, flick the dandruff from my suit . . .
Here they stand and talk, and pout –
Have you read The Tesseract? – *What?* – *Yeah.*
It's even better than The Beach? *He wrote
this one on E, you know?* . . . Unravelling like my coat,
life is in rather poor repair (no, I've not been 'travelling');
they talk, and talk, and – *How adorable!*, a flute
of Krug – just when I can't take another thing,
she calls me over, to help look for her ring,
her ring that simply *must* be found
(but where, in this cluttered waste-ground?),
a souvenir, she says, of some long-dead *affaire* . . .

7.

For the interview, it was herringbone tweed –
what I fancied was a classic literary look
worn (I thought) with postmodern irony.
'I expected someone middle-aged, urbane
and condescending – and I got you.'
Was that double-edged? Over lunch at the Caprice
(her publisher was paying) she told me
how in her twenties, in her time of need
she'd been had 'by half New York', and how
she'd given head until her lips were sore
and I lapped it up. 'Have you *read* my book?'
I had, I heard myself saying, it was a masterpiece
(pornographic, one long howl of pain).
'OK, we're done.' That day, we read no more.

12.

Bracken, brambles, round and round the park, a trek
that used to come as naturally to me
as it now seems forced, theatrical and sad;
hung-over, I can taste the dregs and dreck
of last night's drink, and birdsong is bilious
when it twitters of those things Y said:
stylish, savage, unforgiving (supercilious?),
or of X's line, *tired narcissistic fantasy* . . .
Now it's back to get on with that review,
the latest doorstop Life – by X; beneath the little lamp
in the (temporary) basement room that smells of damp,
the different women differently let down,
the rewind of your life you see before you drown –
how to make all this into something *true*?

13. (Edinburgh)

Up for 'the book thing' in Charlotte Square
I reel away from a shouting-match (or 'Poetry Slam')
and stop dead, realising where I am
and, rooted to the spot, I stare
at that same first-floor bow-window where
after struggling out of heaped blankets, sheets
I parted curtains one long-ago winter morning
to watch the snowfall, while behind me
she stirred among pillows, stretching, yawning
and her eyes seemed to seek me out, and find me . . .
The stillness of those wide white winter streets!
These days, waking up, wanking into a woman
or coming gratefully in her mouth, I feel
I ought to be paying for it (and I am).

EX-POET

Twenty-odd years back, or, if you like, one-third
Through his life (though what did that mean then?)
He took someone's biography at its word
And brought his girlfriend to this sleepy southern town,
To a rented attic where they lay down
Together (dust-motes dancing in shafts of sun),
Where they ate, drank, slept, read, fought
And made up; sometimes he'd rise at dawn
And write, what was more dreamt than thought
In lines that seldom needed honing, the sun-bright
Miracle she was – his love, his muse,
The knowledge he would not betray or lose,
The vision that accompanied him here:
How life can break free of loneliness and fear
To be this richer, riskier thing, like theirs
Who searched for the beautiful and true . . .
At forty-seven (more than two-thirds through,
Or so it seems now), he has come back
To the green flames of cypresses, and palms
Like birds whose tattered, brown-edged feathers
Rustle in the midday heat; to shuttered squares
With fountains dripping moss, and coffee, black
And bitter as the thought of freckled arms
That held him, of her inner weathers,
That he drinks now in the generous shade
Of patched and peeling plane-trees; to the light
He loved then, light that burned his northern eyes
And showed him beauty (or, how all things ache
To be expressed), the truth that what was made
And made well, no-one could unmake.
The girl's long gone. What he wrote were lies.

ONDINE

M'introduire dans ton histoire
C'est en héros effarouché . . .

Mallarmé

Her river was the swift-flowing Rhône;
mine, all that improbable year,
the Hérault ('M'introduire',
I said, 'm'introduire dans ton histoire
c'est en Hérault . . . ') *The two come near*
but do not flow into each other,
any more than the mighty Seine and the Loire.

I walked with her by the mighty Seine and the Loire,
by Fontainebleau, Chambord and Chinon
where the curved neck of a queen carved in stone
trembled in the water, the reflection of a swan
then a real swan sailed by and the moment was gone;
and we were still both there and nowhere,
neither one thing nor the other.

Chopping and changing, neither one thing nor the other
the Blackwater raced over pebbles and a pair
of mermaids basking by the weir,
half-hid in weeds that waved like mermaids' hair;
but you couldn't see beyond it to Cape Clear,
any more than the three sisters, Barrow, Nore and Suir
would ever get to Moscow by way of Rosslare . . .

But what of her whose salt water, whose glair
I tasted by the banks of the Severn, Teme and Yare?
Her whose lips I tasted at Sommières
beside the green Vidourle, where the trout smelt of mud,
she said, loud enough for the fisherman to hear –
whose streams of salt and fresh water, clear
or muddied, laced sometimes with blood

I tasted by the banks of the Deben at the flood,
by the banks of the Mersey, Trent and Humber?
You tasted times without number –
when we ran from the rain splashing in abandoned mugs of beer,
when I said I was leaving, a dutiful daughter
and domes and spires and cranes dissolved to water
while the ferryman waited at the pier.

Now you must believe that I'll appear
at low tide, where mud and water and the estuary
are one, and the ferryman and fisherman both stare
from the little rain-misted jetty out to sea
and it could be her or my mother,
waving, and all flows away from me, from the sheer
cliff-face, leaving gull-cries, torn-off air.

FUGUE

Flow of waterlight. Unbroken blue.
I have come back to a place of healing,
a place of waters, in search of something true,

to heal my life, because *I have not right feeling*
towards women – because I have played
so recklessly, and lost, my mind is reeling

and a solitary gecko in a patch of shade
shows me companionship, and what it is
to sit and wait, and what it is I have made . . .

Farewell to that. Farewell the fond embraces,
farewell the nights in bars, the sunlit walks, the wine
I drank with friends, with Joseph, Gavin, George;

farewell the days I watched light fall on their faces
like a benediction. Peace their portion. Sorrow mine.

                    ❧

This was no place of safety, or place I could call home:
infernal joys, joys of the deadened spirit.
I looked for comfort but no comfort came.

I went to where a tree stood like a flame
that flickered in the petrol-glare; I learnt to fear it.
This was no place of safety, or place I could call home.

Infernal joys of night-time, deadened spirit
on my tongue, my tongue hot as a flame
and the insects uttering their prayer. Who would hear it?

I looked for comfort but no comfort came
on the cold dark tundra, permafrost. My deadened spirit
flickered in the glare of its own shame.

Now everyone is dead, all places are the same.
I looked for comfort but no comfort came.

⁓

A fortress and a harbour wall, a city kneeling
at the mountain's foot as if in penance or in prayer –
the towpath led me here, *au bord de la mer* –

salt glitter, palms like giant bristling birds . . .
All this when I throw back the shutters on my balcony
as on that first morning: out at sea

a vast dazzle, and the terraces filling, petrol-glare
on the boulevards I walk down, mystery-man;
the little island where I skulked like a thief

among the feminists and philosopher-goatherds
who all had their eyes on me, who saw me come to grief
as I watched her move about the deck in her tan,

her little flash of white. The chateau d'If
at sunset. Lust and homesickness. *Not right feeling*.

⁓

Their bodies bloom again from graves in corners.
That sudden writhing – is it maggots, tubers
or, white in moonlight, tangled limbs?

Such trite and terrible visions disturb us . . .
We have come again as mourners
to this funeral, which is ours. The air

tastes of leaf-mould, frogs croak our hymns,
there is a steady murmuring of prayer
from the ruined chapel – that low drone . . .

Patience, patience brings peace, I know. I pray
for patience now, I gather up my dead
and lead them to a place of healing

and one by one they are made whole, myself too
made whole again, by patience. I am grief's prey

~

The kind, the loving hearts go into the cold ground,
into the dark; into dust and ash they go,
and we cannot follow them, or know

to what rest they have gone, what silence found.
I open a window and am lifted clean out, over the lake –
a great light, water-glint, a single swan

gliding over it, and I am lost among gull-cries,
the cries of the heart-broken and the drowned.
Peace to them. They are long gone.

Peace to those who leave the works of hands and ears and eyes,
console us, comfort us, Johannes Vermeer, Brahms.
My father in your dark-room, my mother making cake

you have mixed developing fluid, flour, and I
your orphan, I am in it up to my arms.

A LATE LUNCH

How often, when I walked that path
Between the cows becalmed in the water-meadow
And the chink and rattle of small boats on their moorings,
Or went out into your garden with scissors for rosemary
And stood a moment under the warm wide night and the stars,
I wanted it just to go on and on –
The path, the night, and all of us, together,
The drinks tray waiting and the owl or curlew calling
And that blown rose-bush at the window, so much given back
That I thought I'd lost for ever.

                            Now you're gone
I see you, G&T in hand, in your favourite chair,
Squinting as you take another drag
Or setting out lunch in sunlight on the brand-new deck
You were so proud of, that last summer. Across the creek,
Those sloping fields where a combine harvester
Crawls up and down between the water's edge
And the low horizon; glimpsed through leaves,
The little boathouse, wind-bent sedge
And shingle foreshore, where ebb-tide and flood
Wash gently at old pilings and cormorants share
The winding channels and the shining gull-marked mud –
All just going on and on for ever.

DEDICATIONS, NOTES
AND ACKNOWLEDGEMENTS

'Rotisserie (The Wait)' & '(The Return)': i.m. Ian Hamilton, 1938–2001

'Effects', 'Visit', 'Three-Piece Suite', 'Launderette: Her Last Nightdress' and 'Orpheus': i.m. Deirdre Jenkins (née Herrick), 1925–1997

'Epithalamium': i.m. William Cookson, 1939–2003

'As If': i.m. Kathy Acker, 1945–1997

'Fugue': i.m. Joseph Brodsky, 1940–1995; Gavin Ewart, 1916–1995; George MacBeth, 1932–1992

'A Late Lunch': i.m. Amanda Radice, 1941–2003

The dedicatory poem is a miniature cento, consisting of lines or phrases translated from Rimbaud's 'Le Bateau Ivre', and a line from 'Supreme Death' by Douglas Dunn.

Several other poems adapt or co-opt lines from the following (where not otherwise given, the translations are my own):
   The third part of 'Tales of the Riverbank': Ausonius ('Moselle', etc) in the version by Jack Lindsay
   The last part of 'The Classical Picnic': 'Copa Surisca', a poem in the *Appendix Vergiliana*, in the translation by Helen Waddell
   'Out of Season': 'Scheveningue, Morte Saison' in the *Poésies de A.O. Barnabooth* by Valery Larbaud
   'from *A Shorter Literary Life*, No. 11': 'Complainte Sur Certains Ennuis' by Jules Laforgue

'Epithalamium'
The poems of Barnabooth, the millionaire poet and world-traveller invented by Larbaud, were first published as 'poèmes par un riche amateur' – which to some extent Larbaud at that time was, enjoying a private income from a Vichy water source owned by his family. (He later became a highly professional writer, translator and critic.) In the 1990s, while working on my own translations from Larbaud/Barnabooth, I was a guest of the international translators' centre in Arles. 'Le blanc vierge du papier': the pure – virginal – whiteness of the paper, a phrase not from Larbaud but Mallarmé.

Grateful acknowledgement is made to the editors of the following publications or programmes, in which some of these poems (or earlier versions of them) first appeared or were first broadcast: *Agenda*; *Last Words: New Poetry for the New Century* (Picador); *New Writing 12* (Arts Council of England/British Council); *Poetry Please* (BBC Radio 4); *Poetry Review*; *Pretext 6* (University of East Anglia); *The Forward Book of Poetry, 2002*; *The London Review of Books*; *The Times Literary Supplement*. Seven of the poems were first published in *The Little Black Book* (Cornwall: Cargo Press, 2001).